United States Presidents

Ronald Reagan

Paul Joseph
ABDO Publishing Company

visit us at

www.abdopub.com

Published by Abdo Publishing Company 4940 Viking Drive, Edina, Minnesota 55435.
Copyright © 1998 by Abdo Consulting Group, Inc. International copyrights reserved in
all countries. No part of this book may be reproduced in any form without written
permission from the publisher.

Printed in the United States.

Cover and Interior Photo credits: AP/Wide World, Archive Photos

Edited by Lori Kinstad Pupeza
Contributing editor Brooke Henderson

Library of Congress Cataloging-in-Publication Data

Joseph, Paul, 1970-
        Ronald Reagan / Paul Joseph.
        p. cm. -- (United States presidents)
        Includes index.
        Summary: A biography of the fortieth president of the United States, including
        his childhood, education, employment, and political career.
        ISBN 1-56239-815-6
        1. Reagan, Ronald--Juvenile literature. 2. Presidents--United States--
        Biography--Juvenile literature. [1. Reagan, Ronald. 2. Presidents.] I. Title.
        II. Series: United States presidents (Edina, Minn.)
        E877.J67   1998
        973.917'092--dc21
        [B]   97-44213
                                                                     CIP
                                                                     AC

Contents

President Ronald Reagan 4

Growing Up in Illinois 10

Eureka and the Cubs 12

Ronald Reagan—the Actor 14

The Making of the 40th
United States President 16

Governor Reagan 18

The 40th President 20

The Great Communicator 22

Reagan's Biggest Challenge 26

Fun Facts on President Reagan 28

Glossary 30

Internet Sites 31

Index 32

President Ronald Reagan

*A*t 69 years old, actor turned politician Ronald Reagan was preparing for the biggest role of his life—becoming the president of the United States. He looked much younger than his 69 years and presented himself with confidence. He had a wonderful gift for speaking.

The year was 1980, and a lot of people in America were out of work. A week before the **election**, Ronald Reagan asked the American people during a debate with President Jimmy Carter, "Are you better off than you were four years ago?" Most Americans were not.

The people of America wanted a leader who could take charge and make them feel good about their country again. Ronald Reagan was their man. He took a positive view and declared, "It's morning again in America."

After being the oldest man ever elected president, Reagan went about his job with the energy of a young man. He got the **economy** back on track and created more jobs.

President Ronald Reagan.

Becoming the president of the United States was a long and difficult road for Ronald Reagan. He grew up in Illinois and his family didn't have much money. After graduating from college, Reagan worked in radio and then as an actor.

Reagan later became interested in politics and worked on Harry Truman's campaign for president. At the time, Reagan was a **Democrat**. After a few years he switched parties and became a **Republican**.

Reagan gave up acting and began a full-time career in politics. He was elected governor of California, and later tried to become president of the United States. Reagan ran unsuccessfully two times before being elected the president in 1980.

The road to the White House for Ronald Reagan began in the early 1900s, in a small town in the northwestern part of Illinois.

Opposite page: President Reagan giving a speech.

Ronald W. Reagan (1911-)
Fortieth President

BORN:	February 6, 1911
PLACE OF BIRTH:	Tampico, Illinois
ANCESTRY:	Irish-Scotch-English
FATHER:	John Edward Reagan (1883-1941)
MOTHER:	Nelle Clyde Wilson Reagan (1885-1962)
WIVES:	First wife: Jane Wyman (1914-)
	Second wife: Nancy Davis (1921-)
CHILDREN:	From first wife, Two: 1 boy (adopted), 1 girl
	Second wife, Two: 1 boy, 1 girl
EDUCATION:	Dixon High School; B.A. (1932) Eureka College (Illinois)
RELIGION:	Christian Church
OCCUPATION:	Radio announcer, actor, rancher, businessman
MILITARY SERVICE:	Second Lieutenant, U.S. Army and Army Air Corps; discharged as captain, 1945
POLITICAL PARTY:	Republican

OFFICES HELD: Governor of California; President, Screen Actors Guild; Chairman Motion Picture Industry Council

AGE AT INAUGURATION: 69

TERMS SERVED: Two (1981-1985) (1985-1989)

VICE PRESIDENT: George Bush (both terms)

Detail Area

Tampico

Illinois

Birthplace of Ronald Reagan

Growing Up in Illinois

*R*onald Wilson Reagan was born on February 6, 1911, in the small town of Tampico, Illinois. Ronald was the second of two sons born to John Edward Reagan and Nelle Wilson Reagan. His brother's name was John Neil, who went by his middle name.

The Reagan family did not have much money, but they were very close. Growing up, the brothers were best of friends doing almost everything together. They both loved playing sports and sledding and ice skating.

John was a traveling shoe salesman who moved his family from small town to small town in Illinois. Finally, when young Ronald was nine years old, the family settled in Dixon, Illinois.

Ronald's mother was very close to her two sons. She taught them to read at a very young age. She noticed that Ronald had an excellent memory and could recite word for word many of the readings she had done. Nelle, herself, was an excellent speaker.

Although Ronald was small and nearsighted, he was excellent at sports. He was also an avid swimmer, who held a lifeguard job for several summers. When Ronald entered high school, he showed great interest and terrific talent in three different activities: sports, drama, and politics.

Ronald was on the football and basketball teams in high school and also participated in swimming and track. He had parts in school plays, and was elected the class president of the student council. Ronald was a true leader who had many friends. People in his school, including the teachers, loved his warmth, honesty, leadership, and friendly smile that he gave to anyone who came near.

Reagan as a lifeguard.

Eureka and the Cubs

*A*fter graduating from high school, Ronald attended Eureka College. Like in high school, Ronald was an all-around student. He continued his success in sports, drama, and politics. Ronald was the captain of the swimming team, started on the varsity football team, and was on the track team. As a member of the drama club, he held the lead in many school plays.

Reagan was elected the president of the freshman class. He helped organize a student **strike** against the cutbacks in the college, which led to the president of the college resigning. Ronald was later the president of the entire student body.

Ronald graduated from Eureka in 1932 and got a job as a radio sports announcer in Davenport, Iowa. He was hired to announce the University of Iowa football games for ten dollars a game.

The following year, Reagan got a job at the radio station, WHO, in Des Moines. There Ronald was the radio play-by-play announcer for the Chicago Cubs baseball games.

Although Ronald loved his job, what he really wanted to do was get into show business. His dream was to be in movies. In 1937, while working at the Cubs training camp in California, Ronald got his big break.

Ronald was given a screen test by Warner Brothers—one of the biggest movie studios in the world. Warner Brothers loved his charm, good looks, and acting ability and quickly signed him to a contract for $200 a week. Ronald moved to Hollywood and began an acting career in television and the movies that would span almost 30 years.

Ronald Reagan working as a radio sports announcer in 1932.

Ronald Reagan—the Actor

*A*s a movie actor, Ronald Reagan made more than 50 full-length feature films. His first movie was *Love Is In the Air* in which Ronald played a radio announcer—something he was very used to. Among Ronald's best known movies were *Brother Rat*, *Dark Victory*, and *Knute Rockne—All American*.

While making the movie *Brother Rat* in 1938, Ronald met Jane Wyman. The two were married in 1940. They had a daughter, Maureen Elizabeth, in 1941. In 1945 they adopted their son, Michael Edward. The marriage grew strained, and in 1948, the couple divorced.

During World War II, Ronald was drafted into the military. He was honorably discharged with the rank of captain in 1945.

When Ronald returned from the military he continued to act and also got involved in leadership roles. He became the president of the Screen Actors Guild. Ronald helped achieve better pay, tax relief, and improved working conditions for actors.

In 1952, Ronald married actress Nancy Davis. They had a

daughter, Patricia Ann, who was born in 1952, and a son, Ronald Prescott, who was born in 1958. In 1956, Ronald and Nancy starred in a movie together—*Hellcats of the Navy.*

In 1954, Ronald Reagan began working for General Electric Company as an actor. He also spent several weeks each year speaking to General Electric employees throughout the country. People loved Reagan's speeches and ideas. Ronald knew that he could make a difference in the United States and decided to enter politics.

Ronald (L) and Nancy appearing with Arthur Franz (R) in the 1957 movie Hellcats of the Navy.

The Making of the 40th United States President

1911
Born Feb. 6, in Tampico, Illinois

1920
Family moves to Dixon, IL

1932
Graduates from Eureka College works as a sports announcer in radio

1937
Signs a contract with Warner Bros. Studio to do movies

1945
Adopts son Michael

1947
President of the Screen Actors Guild

1948
Divorces Jane Wyman

1952
Marries Nancy Davis, daughter Patricia is born

1970
Re-elected Governor

1980
Elected President of the United States

1981
Shot in the chest, assassination attempt by John Hinkley, Jr. on March 30

1984
Re-elected President

PRESIDENTIAL

Ronald Reagan

"With all the creative energy at our command, let us begin an era of natural renewal. Let us renew our determination, our courage and our strength . . . We have every right to dream heroic dreams."

➤ 1940 ➤ 1941 ➤ 1942 ➤

Marries Jane Wyman	Daughter Maureen is born	Officer in the U.S. Army Air Corps

Historical Highlights
during Reagan Administration

★ American hostages released from Iran (1981)

★ First female Supreme Court Justice Sandra Day O'Connor appointed (1981)

★ Presidential power passes to George Bush for eight hours (1985)

★ Space Shuttle Challenger explodes (1986)

★ Black Monday Stock Market crash (1987)

➤ 1954 ➤ 1958 ➤ 1966

Television host	Son Ronald is born	Elected Governor of California

1987 **1989** **1994**

Signs Intermediate-Range Nuclear Treaty with the Soviets	George Bush, Vice President, is elected President	Nov. 5th Ronald Reagan reveals he has Alzheimers Disease

YEARS

Governor Reagan

*D*uring the 1940s, Ronald Reagan was a **Democrat**. By 1952, Reagan started believing in **Republican** ideas. He worked on Republican Dwight D. Eisenhower's campaign for president in both the 1952 and 1956 elections.

In 1964, Reagan worked on Barry Goldwater's presidential campaign. Reagan gave an excellent speech for Goldwater. After listening to that speech, people knew that Reagan had a gift for speaking and should run for political office.

With the support of many people Ronald Reagan ran for governor of California in 1966. Although the state had many more Democrats than Republicans, Reagan easily won the **election** by nearly a million votes. The people of California liked Reagan's leadership and re-elected him governor in 1970.

As governor, Reagan had many accomplishments. Both Republicans and Democrats liked him, and he made a name for himself throughout the country. Reagan doubled the amount of money given to schools in California. Reagan knew that education was the key to a good future for young people.

Reagan, an avid outdoorsman, signed the strictest air and water pollution laws in the country. Many states followed his lead by making pollution laws.

People began talking about him as a candidate for president of the United States. Reagan became a candidate in 1968, but lost in the **Republican** primary to Richard Nixon. In 1976, he ran against President Gerald Ford in the Republican primary and lost in a very close contest. As they say, the third time is a charm. And it was a charm in 1980, as the United States began the Reagan Revolution.

Ronald Reagan greeting supporters while campaigning for governor.

The 40th President

*I*n July 1980, at the **Republican** Convention, the Republicans nominated Ronald Reagan as their presidential candidate. Reagan chose George Bush as his vice president.

Reagan was running against President Jimmy Carter. Carter was having a very difficult time running the United States. **Inflation** was high, unemployment was high, and Carter's overall approval rating was low.

Carter knew he would have a difficult time beating Reagan so he decided to poke fun at Reagan's acting background. Reagan's experience, however, before the cameras and microphones gave him poise, timing, and control that people liked.

In November of 1980, Ronald Reagan, at 69 years old, became the oldest man ever elected as president of the United States. At his victory celebration Reagan announced, "We're going to put Americans back to work again."

Just two months into his presidency, on March 30, 1981, Ronald Reagan was shot by an **assassin**. John Hinckley, Jr., fired six shots at the president outside a Washington, D.C. hotel. A police officer, a Secret Service agent, and the White House press secretary were also struck. A bullet entered President Reagan's left side and lodged in his lung, just an inch away from his heart.

Reagan was rushed to a nearby hospital, where doctors performed emergency surgery to remove the bullet from his chest. Reagan made a full recovery and even joked with the doctors at the hospital saying, "I hope you guys are **Republicans**." President Reagan's strength, courage, and humor under such serious circumstances made him a hero to many Americans.

President Reagan working in the Oval Office.

The Great Communicator

*R*onald Reagan was greatly applauded for his appointment of Sandra Day O'Connor to the Supreme Court. She became the first woman in the history of the United States to become a Supreme Court justice. He also chose two women for his **cabinet**: Elizabeth Dole and Margaret Heckler.

President Reagan also stopped a **strike** by air-traffic controllers. As government employees, they legally cannot strike. "The law is the law, and the law says they cannot strike," he said. He fired those who did not return to work.

By the presidential **election** of 1984, Reagan was more popular than ever. The **economy** was great and people were back to work. Reagan won a huge victory on November 6, 1984, in the presidential election.

President Reagan won every state over Democratic challenger Walter Mondale, except Mondale's own state of Minnesota. After the huge victory, Speaker of the House Tip O'Neill, a **Democrat**, declared that "Reagan is the most popular figure in the history of the United States."

Ronald Reagan, with wife Nancy at his side, is sworn in as president for the second time in January of 1985.

In 1986, President Reagan's popularity began to fall because of a secret plan known as the Iran-Contra scandal. The Reagan **Administration** sold military supplies to the Iran government in hopes that they would release American hostages who were being held by terrorists in the country of Lebanon. It was all a secret plan.

President Reagan, himself, said he did not know anything about the secret plan. Many Americans did not believe him and his popularity dropped.

One of Ronald Reagan's greatest accomplishments was the work he did with Soviet Union leader Mikhail Gorbachev. In 1987, the two leaders signed the Intermediate-Range **Nuclear** (INF) Treaty. This treaty called for the destruction of many nuclear missiles. It was considered by people all over the world as a wonderful accomplishment because for many years the United States and Soviet Union were not on good terms.

President Reagan got the treaty signed because he was able to work hard, make friends with former enemies, and communicate his ideas. In the United States he went by a nickname for many years and, after signing the treaty, other countries even referred to him as "The Great Communicator."

Reagan and Gorbachev exchange copies of the INF Treaty.

Reagan's Biggest Challenge

*O*n January 20, 1989, Ronald Reagan was pleased to hand over the presidency to his vice president and good friend, George Bush. Bush defeated **Democrat** Michael Dukakis. Reagan and his wife Nancy flew home to California to finally retire.

The couple spent most of their time at their ranch relaxing and riding horses. Reagan also kept busy writing his memoirs.

Gifted with charm, good looks, and the reputation as "the great communicator," even nearing his 80s, Reagan was in high demand to give speeches in the United States and around the world. In Japan, Reagan received over two million dollars to visit and speak.

Ronald Reagan, the always positive and energetic leader, who worked hard and used his talents to achieve the highest office in the land, would face his most difficult challenge after his presidency.

On November 5, 1994, Ronald Reagan revealed that he had Alzheimer's disease. The main symptoms of Alzheimer's are memory loss, mental disorientation (this means you don't know who you are or where you are), and diminishing health, which leads to death.

In a written statement, Reagan told the world of his illness. He wanted to make his sickness public so people would be aware of the disease, would understand it, and hopefully someday find a cure.

President Bill Clinton called the former president a true hero who not only devoted himself to helping people when he was president, but also in the most private of personal times after his presidency.

Ronald Reagan, who gave the country hope in desperate times, declared in his final written statement, "I have begun the journey that will lead me into the sunset of my life."

Ronald Reagan at his ranch with Russian leader Mikhail Gorbachev.

Fun Facts on President Reagan

•Ronald Reagan loved jelly beans so much that he had to have them with him wherever he went. The jelly beans that Reagan liked, known as "Jelly Bellies," became a craze in the United States.

•Reagan was the first president to appoint a woman to the Supreme Court. In 1981, he appointed Sandra Day O'Connor.

•President Reagan and his brother Neil each were given nicknames growing up that they kept for life. Ronald's was "Dutch" and Neil's was "Moon."

•Ronald Reagan was the first president to wear contact lenses.

•While covering the Chicago Cubs professional baseball team, Reagan suffered a technical difficulty. He was not at the game but getting the game through a ticker tape. The ticker tape broke down. While it was being fixed Ronald continued broadcasting the game by faking it. He joked that a player fouled off a ball 23 times in-a-row! When it was fixed he found out the man grounded to first and ended the inning.

•Ronald Reagan was both a television and movie actor. His most famous role was that of the "Gipper" in the football movie: *Knute Rockne—All American.*

Ronald Reagan acting in the movie, Knute Rockne—All American.

Glossary

Administration—the entire staff that works for a president.

Assassin—a person that murders or tries to murder a very important person.

Cabinet—a group of people picked by a president who are his advisers. They help him run the country.

Democrat—one of the two main political parties in the United States. Democrats are known to be more liberal and believe in more government.

Economy—in government this has to do with the employment rate, interest rate, and producing and buying of products. The United States economy is one of the biggest concerns to the people of America.

Election—a process where people can vote for a public official.

Inflation—when there is an increase in money and credit, which makes the prices of everyday products rise.

Inaugural—the first day that a person is sworn into a political office.

Nuclear—power that is charged through atomic energy.

Republican—one of two main political parties in the United States. Republicans are known to be more conservative and believe in less government.

Senate—also known as congress, is a group of 100 elected senators (two from each state) that represent their state and make laws for the country.

Strike—to quit working because of unfair job policies.

Internet Sites

United States Presidents Information Page
http://we.got.net/docent/soquel/prez.htm
Links to information about United States Presidents. This site is very informative, with biographies on every president as well as speeches and debates, and other links.

The Presidents of the United States of America
http://www.whitehouse.gov/WH/glimpse/presidents/html/presidents.html
This site is from the White House. With an introduction from President Bill Clinton and biographies that include each president's inaugural address, this site is excellent. Get White House History information, Art in the White House, First Ladies, First Families, and much more.

POTUS—Presidents of the United States
http://www.ipl.org/ref/POTUS/
In this resource you will find background information, election results, cabinet members, presidency highlights, and some odd facts on each of the presidents. Links to biographies, historical documents, audio and video files, and other presidential sites are also included to enrich this site.

These sites are subject to change. Go to your favorite search engine and type in United States Presidents for more sites.

Pass It On

History Enthusiasts: educate readers around the country by passing on information you've learned about Presidents or other important people who've changed history. Share your little-known facts and interesting stories. We want to hear from you!

To get posted on the ABDO Publishing Company website E-mail us at "History@abdopub.com"
Visit the ABDO Publishing Company website at www.abdopub.com

Index

A

Alzheimer's disease 26
assassin 20

B

Bush, George 9, 20, 26

C

cabinet 22
Carter, Jimmy 4, 20
Chicago Cubs 13, 28
college 6, 12

D

Davis, Nancy 8, 14
Democrat 6, 18, 22, 26
Dole, Elizabeth 22

E

economy 4, 22
Eisenhower, Dwight D. 18
election 4, 18, 22
Eureka College 12, 16

F

Ford, Gerald 19

G

Goldwater, Barry 18
Gorbachev, Mikhail 24
governor of California
    6, 18
Great Communicator
    22, 24, 26

H

Hinckley, John Jr. 20

I

Illinois 6, 8, 10
Iowa 12
Iran-Contra scandal 24

J

jelly beans 28

M

military service 8
Mondale, Walter 22
movies 13, 14

N

Nixon, Richard 19
nuclear missiles 24

P

politician 4
pollution laws 19

R

radio sports announcer 12
Reagan, Nelle Wilson 10
Republican 6, 8, 18, 19,
    20, 21

S

Sandra Day O'Connor
    22, 28
school 11, 12, 18
Soviet Union 24

T

Truman, Harry 6

W

Warner Brothers 13
Washington, D.C. 21
White House 6, 21
World War II 14
Wyman, Jane 8, 14